ANIMALS
Have Families

by Nadia Ali

PEBBLE
a capstone imprint

Published by Pebble, an imprint of Capstone
1710 Roe Crest Drive, North Mankato, Minnesota 56003
capstonepub.com

Library of Congress Cataloging-in-Publication Data is available on the Library of Congress website.

ISBN: 9780756571849 (hardcover)
ISBN: 9780756571795 (paperback)
ISBN: 9780756571801 (ebook PDF)

Summary: A baby kangaroo lives in its mother's pouch. A zebra group is called a dazzle. A mother octopus has thousands of babies! Find out how animal families care for their young, keep one another safe, and share duties.

Editorial Credits:
Editor: Kristen Mohn; Designer: Tracy Davies; Media Researcher: Svetlana Zhurkin; Production Specialist: Katy LaVigne

Image Credits:
Alamy: Nature Picture Library, 13; Dreamstime: Bo Jonsson, 16; Getty Images: GlobalP, 18, Jeff Foott, 7, JunYi Chow, 28, merrilyanne, 14, Mike Hill, cover, Robert Muckley, 19, Stuart Westmorland, 10; Newscom: Xinhua News Agency/Xinhua, 9; Shutterstock: Anh Luu, 20, beltsazar, 29, Cathy Keifer, 24, Claudio Bertolon, 8, David Cochelin, 17, David James Thomson, 26, isabel kendzior, 1, 11, Jo Crebbin, 4, knelson20, 23, ktoshka_vi, 22, L Galbraith, 5, Michael J Thompson, 21, robert mcgillivray, 12, Savo Ilic, 25, slowmotiongli, 6, Uw.Art, 15, vkilikov, 27

TABLE OF CONTENTS

Words in **bold** are in the glossary.

Animal Families

People have families. So do animals! Like human babies, animal babies all begin with families.

Some families are big. Some are small. Together they protect, hunt, and look after each other. Let's find out how animal families live in the wild!

Super Moms

Elephants live in a group called a **herd**. The oldest and biggest female is the leader. She is the **matriarch**. She finds food and water. She keeps the herd safe. Females in the herd work together to help care for the babies.

A mother orca whale looks after
her baby and other babies in the **pod**.
She feeds her **calf** milk and protects it.
When the calf is about two years old,
the mother gives it hunting lessons.

A baby kangaroo is called a joey. It lives in a special pouch on its mother's belly. The joey stays near its mother for about a year. Then it hops away to live on its own.

A giant panda is large. But its baby is very small! The mother holds the tiny cub in her arms for weeks. She feeds it and keeps it warm. She gently carries the cub in her mouth when she's on the go.

eggs

octopus

The giant Pacific octopus is the largest octopus in the ocean. A mother has about 50,000 eggs at once! She protects them from **predators** until they hatch. Then the babies, called **larvae,** swim away.

Look, twin cubs! Most polar bear mothers have two babies at once. The mother keeps her cubs safe and warm in a den under the snow and ice. After about 12 weeks, she takes them out to explore!

Daddy Duty

A mother emperor penguin lays an egg. Then she leaves on a long hunting trip. The father protects the egg until it hatches. He takes care of the chick until the mother returns with her belly full!

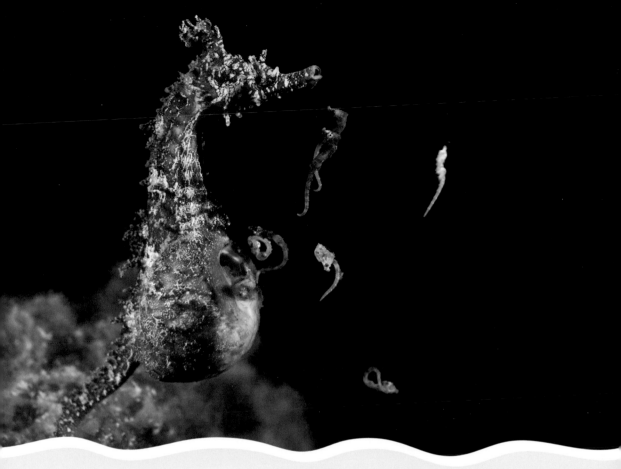

Sea horses are different from most animals. Instead of mothers, it is fathers that give birth. Large sea horses may have up to 2,000 tiny babies!

The father carries them in a special pouch. After they are born, baby sea horses take care of themselves.

A father red fox takes care of his family. The mother and pups stay in the den. The father hunts and brings food to them. As the pups grow, they will learn to hunt.

A father clownfish creates a nest. The mother lays eggs—as many as 1,000!

The father fans the eggs with his fins. This helps the eggs **survive**. In about 10 days, the eggs hatch. Then the baby fish are on their own.

eggs

Marmosets are born in twos. The father helps look after the twins. He cleans the babies. He carries them on his back until they are stronger. He shows them good foods to eat. Baby monkeys have a lot to learn!

A father ostrich protects his eggs with feathers! His dark feathers help to hide the eggs at night. He also protects his chicks by **luring** predators away from the nest.

Big Families

Gorillas live together in a group called a **troop**. A troop may have about 30 gorillas. Gorillas take care of others in their troop. They play during the day. They sleep at night. Just like you!

Roar! A **pride** of lions has about 15 mothers, a couple of fathers, and their young. A mother will fight to protect the cubs in her pride. The mothers chase and hunt prey to feed the pride.

Grunt, grunt! That's the sound of a big herd of bison. Up to 200 females and their young live together. They are always on the move, eating grass. They run when danger is near.

Female alligators and their **hatchlings** live in a group called a congregation. They hang out near the water and wait for food to come by. Mothers carry their young on their back. Hop on!

Look up in a cave! Mother bats and their babies live in a group called a colony. Mothers fly with babies hanging on. The bats look after each other. They chirp loudly! Together, they stay safe.

A dazzle is a group of zebras. Their stripes dazzle the eyes! One father and many mothers and their young live in a dazzle. They run in zigzags when chased. If a predator gets close, a zebra kicks hard!

Changing Children

A butterfly is a colorful, winged insect. But when it is born, it looks very different. The larva looks like a worm! It is a caterpillar. In a few weeks, it changes into a butterfly.

A young frog is not a frog yet. It's a larva called a tadpole. A tadpole looks a bit like a fish. It begins to grow legs after many weeks. Then it starts to look more like its mother and father. Hop, hop!

A baby swan is called a cygnet. It has gray or brown feathers and short wings. The fuzzy feathers help keep cygnets warm. In a year or more, they will grow white feathers.

Dolphins are **mammals**. Like many mammal babies, young dolphins look like their parents but smaller.

A dolphin may stay in its pod for years. Playing, hunting, clicking, and whistling!

A silvered leaf monkey is also a mammal. It has silvery gray hair. But its babies are orange! The bright color helps mothers spot their babies. After a few months, the baby's hair turns gray.

A baby sea turtle hatches on a beach. More than 100 hatch at once. They all run for the ocean!

After they grow, females may return to the same beach. They are ready to lay eggs of their own!

Glossary

calf (kaf)—a young animal such as a whale or elephant

hatchling (HACH-ling)—an animal that has recently hatched from an egg

herd (HURD)—a large group of animals that lives or moves together

larva (LAR-vuh)—the early form of an animal, such as a frog, that looks very different from its parents; more than one larva are larvae (LAR-vee)

lure (LEWR)—to make an animal come away or toward something

mammal (MAMM-uhl)—a warm–blooded animal that breathes air; mammals have hair or fur; female mammals feed milk to their young

matriarch (MAY-tree-ark)—the female leader of a group

pod (POD)—a group of animals, such as dolphins or whales

predator (PREH-duh-tur)—an animal that hunts other animals for food

pride (PRYDE)—a group of lions

survive (ser-VYVE)—to stay alive

troop (TROOP)—a group or flock of mammals or birds

Read More

Ali, Nadia. *Animals Live in Homes*. North Mankato, MN: Capstone, 2023.

Eszterhas, Suzi. *Baby Animals with Their Families*. Berkeley, CA: Owlkids Books, Inc., 2019.

Salas, Laura Purdie. *Meet My Family! Animal Babies and Their Families*. Minneapolis: Millbrook Press, 2018.

Internet Sites

Enchanted Learning: Names of Animals, Babies, and Groups
enchantedlearning.com/painting/Animalbabies.shtml

National Geographic Kids: Animal Types
kids.nationalgeographic.com/animals

PBS Kids: Animal Games
pbskids.org/games/animals

Index

About the Author

Nadia Ali is a children's book author. She writes in various genres and is especially fond of animals. Inspired by her kitty, Cici, she contributes pet articles and features to magazines and websites. Nadia was born in London and currently resides in the Caribbean, where she happily swapped out London's gray skies for clear blue skies. She lives with her husband and has two married daughters.